Streams & Dreams & Fairy Queens

MELODY HAMBY GOSS

AuthorHouse™
1663 Liberty Drive
Bloomington, IN 47403
www.authorhouse.com
Phone: 1 (800) 839-8640

Published by AuthorHouse 02/06/2019

ISBN: 978-1-5462-7844-3 (sc)
ISBN: 978-1-5462-7845-0 (e)

Print information available on the last page.

This book is printed on acid-free paper.

authorHOUSE®

Streams & Dreams
Fairy Queens

For Gwen

Contents

You may say I'm a dreamer but I'm not the only one, I hope some day you'll join us and the world will be as one...John Lennon

"A Bridge Of Flowers"

(Build bridges not walls)

*Greet each man with peace, and leave each man with love…ask
yourself – one more enemy, or one more dove? Suzy Kassem*

Croaked the frog to bumble bee,
Away you fly away from me…
Venture not my pond my home,
With stripp'd yellow wings
You roam…

Belongs to we the croaking frogs,
Cattails grow in ponds and bogs…
In your hives in forest stay,
We need you not so fly
Away…

You silly frog laughs the bee,
In no ponds by woodland tree…
Lily pads no longer grow,
Ponds and lakes no
Longer flow…

Behind your wall on pads you lie,
Lest you croak when cattails die…
Need we all this world of ours,
With bridges built
Of fragrant
Flowers…

A bumblebee or croaking frog,
In woodland tree or swampy bog…
Forms a bridge with flowers bright,
While frogs they sing to
Bees delight…

Life is like a pond, and every decision and act we commit, good or bad, is a pebble flung nto it…the ripples spread in widening circles…Francine Rivers

"A Frog Story"

If life were easy, it wouldn't be difficult...Kermit the Frog

A frog there sat with blackened eye,
On lily pad both him and I...
Face downcast ashamed was he,
"Not what you think" he said
To me...

"Night of last were butterflies,
In silence here to them I spied...
My tongue I licked while waiting here,
But out they flew to
Meadows near"...

"Stomach growling empty still,
A buzzing heard from yonder hill...
How sweetly fair this fattened fly,
My tongue lashed out, he
Didn't die"...!

"A wayward tick and drunken flee,
With that fly all tackled me...
By my pads of lilies green,
Flew butterflies with
Wings unseen"...

"Thrashing round from here and there,
Flying fist and wings in air...
Out flew a pretty butterfly,
Hard she smacked me
In my eye"...

"So...on my lily pad am I,
With a badly blackened eye...
Future meals no meat for me,
A vegan frog now on
I'll be"...

Nature is my church, the wind in the trees and the bugs and the frogs, all those things are comfort to me…Sissy Spacek

"A Prince Unseen"

It wasn't a kiss that changed the frog, but the fact that a young girl looked beneath warts and slime and believed she saw a prince…so h became one…Richelle E. Goodrich

Beneath her cloak a robe of white,
A damsel there in shadowed light…
Hearing songs by distant frogs,
To them her head she
Kindly nods…

Green are gems in raven hair,
Her prince she seeks this damsel fair…
Frogs they sing so faint and sweet,
Fearing please her prince
To meet…

In shadowed light this damsel fair,
With crying eyes and thoughts despair…
Beneath her cloak a robe of white.
Her prince she seeks in
Distant light…

Faint and sweet a frog unseen,
His hands he holds a gem of green…
A damsel there in shadowed mist,
Before her bowing please
To kiss…

Hearing songs of distant frogs,
To him, her prince she kindly nods…
With raven hair and gems of green,
Nevermore the frog
Unseen…

In storybooks and damsels fair,
Of singing frogs where princes dare…
Seeking not the gems of green,
Pursuing but their prince
Unseen…

They beat their swords upon their shields, to no beast or man would they yield…Muse, Enigmatic Evolution

"A Tarnished Crown"

My task set before me, girl, my mission clear and true. There'll be black knights
and dragons, girl, but I will always come for you…Emme Rollins

Drowsy eyed this book I read,
Of gallant knights and mighty steeds…
Sweet maidens fair with golden hair,
A captive there in ol 'Kings
Lair…

Through my door a stately queen,
Cheeks blushed bright with eyes of green…
Rustles from her sapphire gown,
Her hand held tight a
Tarnished crown…

Ceasing sobs through my door,
A gallant knight o'er the moors…
A captive once in ol' King's lair,
With eyes of green and
Golden hair…

Awake at last still drowsy eyed,
This book I read still by my side…
My lap their lays a sapphire gown,
By my feet a tarnished
Crown…

Few humans see fairies or hear their music, but many find fairy rings of dark grass, scattered with toadstools, left by their dancing feet...Judy Allen

"As The Fairies Fly"

In a few blinks you can almost see the fairies moving in…but first you
can almost hear the crackle of their wings…Vera Nazarian

Yon hills of green beyond me sleep,
Through darkest windowpanes I peep…
Where fairies frolic o'er the land,
Beneath my window
Hand in hand…

Fluttered wings 'neath diamond skies,
Shadows tiny as they fly…
O'er hills of green in best attire
Dancers all in nature's
Choir…

Sleepy-eyed my dreams are nigh,
As hand in hand the fairies fly…
Dancing yet to nature's choir,
Flying they in best
Attire…

Through darkest windowpanes I peep,
Eyes no longer closed in sleep…
O'er the hills of green I sing,
Flying as the fairies
Wing…

'Neath diamond studded darkest sky,
With fairies tiny now
I fly…

Be led by the dreams in your
heart...Roy T. Bennett

"Asleep I Dream"

I dream. Sometimes I think that's the only right thing to do…Haruki Murakumi

On a camel have you rode,
Or sweetly kissed the lips of toads…
Lived as a painted butterfly,
While fluttering o'er the
Meadows nigh…

On a rose with petals red,
There you lay in garden's bed…
Cheerful they the flowers please,
Unseen beneath the winter's
Freeze…

With a tiger have you walked,
Or with a parrot there you talked…
Howling with gray wolves each night,
Shadowed there in silvered
Light…

On a dolphin did you ride,
Beneath the sea at ebbing tide…
Fishes they all fade away,
Unknown poor fish where
Dolphins play…

Each of these at evenings nigh,
All I've done when daylight dies…
With wolves I howl in silvered light,
My eyes wide-shut in dreams
Each night…

A dreamer yes, and always be,
Where lions talk and walk
With me…

I heard the bells on Christmas day,
their old familiar carols play. And
wild and sweet the words repeat…
of peace on Earth, good will to men!…
Henry Wadsworth Longfellow

"Christmas Mouse Again"

And, so, Christmas comes to bless us! Comes to teach us how to find, the joy of
giving happiness and the joy of being kind…Gertrude Tooley Buckingham

In my dream-state worrying,
O'er my head feet scurrying…
One eye awake while listening,
A sound like now he's
Whistling…

Hoping last year he had died,
With that trap of cheese I plied…!
Now in the attic moving in,
This Christmas mouse I'll kill
Again…!

By my tree of Christmas green,
Nibbling there on crumbs unseen…
To me he smiles with yellow'd lips,
With crumbs of cheese again
He slips…!

Grabbing cheese again I ply,
Traps with springs I hope he'll die..
In the attic on the stairs,
Traps with cheese are
Everywhere…!

Again I lay upon my bed,
With sneer on lips I lay my head…
Snap..!! I hear on attic stair,
Dead I know he's
Laying there…!

Wide awake this Christmas eve,
Toward the attic steps I leave…
Gone are traps with cheese I plied,
On attic steps no mouse
Has died…

By Christmas Tree of green I sat,
Wondering "where in heaven is that rat"?
Spying traps with ribbons bright,
A written note from mouse
This night…

"To my friend this Christmas Eve"
I'm leaving not so do not grieve…
Thank you for the traps of cheese,
From Walmart always buy
Them please…!

Beneath my tree are mice at play,
While hearing bells this
Christmas Day…!

Talk of an angel and you'll hear their wings…Proverbs

"Cry Not The Angels"

When angels visit us, we do not hear the rustle of their wings, nor feel the feathery touch of the breast of a dove; but we know their presence by the love they create in our hearts…Mary Baker Eddy

Bright the stars in silver shine,
Standing angels wings entwined…
Blare of trumpets mourn the night,
Stands the angels winged
With light…

Cry not the angles wings entwined,
An angel new in silver shines…
Silent sings his trumpet's sound,
An angel new with wings
Unbound…

Cry not the angels standing there,
An angel new on heaven's stair…
Light of stars forever shine,
Each one an angel wings
Entwined…

Cry not the mortals faded form,
Tonight an angel newly born…
Unbound wings now entwined,
As bright the stars in
Silver shine…

Cry not the mortals faded form,
Tonight an angel newly
Born…

A garden to walk in and immensity to dream in – what more could we ask? A few flowers at our feet and above us the stars…Victor Hugo

"Dancing With Dandelions"

I will be the gladdest thing under the sun; I will touch a hundred
flowers and not pick one…Edna St. Vincent Mallay

Pale waters thick with lily pads awake in mornings' blue,
Unfurled roses crimson red where violets shy once grew…
Rods of golden yellow in mountains wild and free,
Dance with dandelions and woodland's
Honey'd bee…

Pansies purle'd red and blue scent dawning's early hour,
As angels wing'd sing praises to natures' passion-flower…
Daisies white with slender stems sway by forest stream,
On fragrant windswept breezes scenting
Summers' green…

While bells of blue by myrtle trees beckon butterflies,
Angels wing'd sing praises 'neath dawnings' purple skies…
Flower's all and everyone unnamed and left to grow,
Scent morning's early hours when windswept
Breezes blow…

Pale waters thick, with lily-pads, wake in mornings' blue,
As dandelions yellow dance where violets

Shy once grew…

The wall is silence, the grass is sleep,
tall trees of peace their vigil keep. And
the Fairy of Dreams with moth-wings
furled plays soft on her flute to the
drowsy world…Ida Rentoul Outhwaite

"Faint & Fair The Fairy"

The fairy poet takes a sheet of moonbeams silver-white' His ink is dew
from daisies sweet, his pen a point of light...Joyce Kilmer

By the stream a fairy amid wild daffodils,
Soft of voice she's speaking in a woodland still…
Slender stemmed the daisies scenting everywhere,
O'er the streambed watching squirrels
From over there…

Passing by a sparrow winging on his way,
Through the willows singing waving feathers gray…
Endearing woodland fairy in a forest still,
Soft of voice she's speaking amid
Wild daffodils…

Faint and fair the fairy tiny by the steam,
Dust of glitter falling melting into dreams…
Wait the sparrow singing by scented daisies there,
For the fairy tiny silver faint
And fair…

In my bed awaking a fragrance everywhere,
Fall of glitter dusting sparkles in the air…
Faint and fair a fairy on a sparrow gray,
Through my window singing
Winging on their way…

Softly scented daisies on my windowsill,
While in my hair entangled were

Tiny daffodils…

The fairy poet takes a sheet of
moonbeam, silver white; His ink
is dew from daisies sweet, his pen
a point of light...Joyce Kilmer

"Footprints Of Fairies"

Fairies are invisible and inaudible like angels, but their magic sparkles in nature…Lynn Holland

Far off hills in mornings I've seen,
Kissing of meadows by forests green…
Mist covered streams clouding the dale,
Earth's spiritual songs
Echo as well…

Wake they the flowers in morning's mist,
Eyes golden winking Earth Fairies kissed…
Silver lined footprints left here and there,
Kissing the meadows where no
Mortals dare…

Shoes tiny pointed covered in dew,
Fluttering wings of turquoise with blue…
Jealous the angels where no mortals dare,
Of footprints the fairies leave
Here and there…

Silver the dew each morning is seen,
In meadows once kissed by forest of green…
Wink they the flowers covered in dew,
By fluttering fairies of turquoise
And blue…

Jealous the angels where no mortals dare,
Of footprints the fairies leave
Here and there…

You can't make a frog richer who already has a great sun and a pretty lake with green leaves, insects and flowers! He is already the richest of the rich!...Mehmet Murat ildan

"From Lily Pad To Lily Pad"

A frog in a little pond can be much happier than a fish in a vast ocean!...Mehmet Murat ildan

Lily pad to lily pad jumps a frog alone,
Lily pad to lily pad searching for a home…
Far away his parents bog by a forest stream,
Croaking frogs in unison once his
Happy dream…

Flies of fire flying 'round the swampy bogs,
From lily pad to lily pad by decaying logs…
Trees of cypress swaying to pelicans display,
Shades of twilights wandering where
Alligators lay…

Jumps the frog to empty log finally is he,
Home again happy searching for a she…
From lily pad to lily pad spies a frog alone,
In shades of twilights wanderings
Searching for her home…

Croaking frogs in unison sing a happy song,
Lily pad to lily pad now
Where they belong…

Want to keep Christ in Christmas? Feed the hungry, clothe the naked forgive the guilty, welcome the unwanted, care for the ill, love your enemies, and do unto others as you would have done unto you….Steve Maraboli

"In Lands Where Children Play"

Then the Grinch thought of something he hadn't before! What if Christmas, he thought, doesn't come from a store. What if Christmas...perhaps...means a little bit more!...Dr. Seuss

Evergreens and mistletoe candy-canes red swirled,
Wrapped gifts awaiting Christmas for little boys and girls...
Jingle bells with fairy tales scenes of Santa's sleigh,
Trees whisper "Merry Christmas" in lands
Where children play...

Gentle blowing snow of white glistens here and there,
Elves in Santa's toyshop complete with teddy bear...
Choo-choo trains and dolly's packed in Santa's sleigh,
Trees whisper "Merry Christmas" in lands
Where children play...

Suit of red with blackened boots whiskers grayish white,
"Ho-Ho-Ho" his laughter on Christmas Eve tonight...
Evergreens and mistletoe candy-canes red swirled,
Past the north-star flying for little
Boys and girls...

A teddy-bear for Johnny, baby Susie's rattle pink,
Past the North star flying to all a tearful wink...
Across the border sadly no candy-canes swirled red,
No toys for children crying, hungry
In their beds...

Head bowed low and saddened, whiskers grayish-white,
Faraway a Christmas tree whispers in the night...
Border-walls in darkness hear Jingle bells at play,
Bright-eyed boys and little girls
Wait for Santa's
Sleigh...

Past the North-Star flying Santa's heading home,
Sleigh half-filled with presents...
Another year

Alone...

Every great dream begins with a dreamer. Always remember, you have within you the strength, the patience, the passion to reach for the stars to change the world…Harriet Tubman

"My Sweet Arise"

You may say I'm a dreamer but I'm not the only one. I hope someday
you'll join us, and the world will live as one...John Lennon

In antique lands where childhood dreams,
Where flowers dance on blue sunbeams…
As dragons fly in shadowed light,
With robins red and
Rabbits white…

Deer of brown by babbling streams,
In antique lands where childhood dreams…
Pink poppies play with golden eyes,
Begging child,
"My sweet arise"…

On dragon's silver arrowed tail,
Through meadows fly in flowered vale…
Kissing girls while dreaming nigh,
"My sweet arise, with
Violet eyes"…

My darling sleep with wide-shut eyes,
Dream your dreams where dragons fly…
With violets red and rabbits white,
On sunbeams dance in sparkled
Light…

The butterfly counts not months
but moments, and has time
enough…Rabindranth Tagore

"Nature's Attire"

The Earth has music for those that listen

Glad of nature gives me peace,
A simple howl of wolf's release…
Chirping birds in forest green,
Earth's sunsets red lie
In-between…

Grows the grass on yonder hill,
Willows weep and weep they will…
Mountain tops with covered snow,
Valleys deep way
Below…

With kindred eye a sparrow sings,
Sainted bird of feathered wings…
Mourn the doves each dawning day,
In forest green where
Coyotes play…

Floating still on morning winds,
White the clouds as day begins…
Drops of dew on flowers red,
Wash petals sweet in
Garden's bed…

Wake your eyes to nature's choir,
Dressed she is in fine attire…
Howls the wolf at close of day,
In forest green where
Coyotes play…

Come away, O human child to the waters
wet and wild, with a fairy, hand in hand,
for the world's more full of weeping than
you can understand…William Butler Yeats

"On Silvered Wings Of Sunshine"

In a few blinks you can almost see the fairies moving in…but first,
you hear the crackle of their wings…Vera Nazarian

On a flower yellow a fairy tiny plays,
Wings of silver sunshine with fairy tiny ways…
Shoes pointed painted purple hair a golden hue,
Eyes of violet color shining in
The dew…

From my place in hiding, watching fairy play,
On a flower yellow with fairy tiny ways…
Silvered wings of sunshine sparkled in the dew,
While on the flower playing her hair
A golden hue…

Hiding still I listen a humming tune I hear,
Sweetly-faint her music playing in my ear…
Fluttered wings of sunshine silent in the air,
Towards the forest flying tiny soft
And fair…

Sadly by the flower a yellow fragrant scent,
Hearing still her humming fairy tiny went…
Wings of silver sunshine wonderful to see,
Towards the forest flying waving
Back at me…

Because you tread on my dreams,
the world is made of magic things...
David Paul Kilpatrick

"Once Time Forgot"

Darkness is not forever; eventually there will be stars…David Paul Kilpatrick

In moonshine there a shadow weeps,
With golden crown and sandaled feet…
Maiden sweet in nightly air,
Still she waits by
Castle stair…

Dim is the light from ivied tower,
Low burns her lamp this midnight hour…
The friar's steps on cobblestone,
With rustling robes on
Stairs alone…

Gray of beard and wrinkled eyes,
By castle stair he bids goodbye…
In moonshine weeps a maiden sweet,
With golden crown and
Sandaled feet…

A wedding feast with-in the walls,
Though by the stairs her lover calls…
On cobblestones the friar keeps,
As maiden there no longer
Weeps…

By the sea from ivied tower,
On stead her knight this midnight hour…
Away they ride to Camelot,
In moonshine there
Once time
Forgot…

Fairies with gossamer wings, bring forth beauty, grace and joyful things. Fairies of Earth are caretakers of our soil, water and trees…they watch over beautiful creatures such as bears, bunnies, and bees…. appreciate the place from which you stand, then trod carefully each step you make across this land….Molly Friedenfeld

"Outside My Window"

Come away, O human child! To the waters and the wild, with a faery, hand in hand…
for the world's more full of weeping than you can understand…W.B. Yeats

Outside my window watching
Paused fairies in the dew…
Silvered wings of magic,
Shimmered as they
Flew…

Through each shadow nightly,
Bright the moon may be…
Ghost-like wild their spirit,
As fairies flying
Free…

Beneath my window faintly,
Wings fluttered silver-gray…
As a whispered echo,
Whisking me
Away…

Through your window peeking,
While looking right at you…
Ghost-like is my spirit,
Pausing in the
Dew…

Through each shadow nightly.
Bright the moon may be…
With wings of silver'd magic
As a fairy flying
Free…

I am longing to be with you, and by the sea, where we can talk together freely and build our castles in the air…Bram Stoker, Dracula

"Silent Swaying Seaweed"

We are like islands in the sea, separate on the surface but connected in the deep

A little fish beneath the sea a bigger fish yet to be,
Reefs of colored corral all are home to me…
Treasures under ocean by the ebbing tide,
Through shinning turquoise waters on
Turtles back I ride…

In silent swaying seaweed by corral all aglow,
Another fish so little hiding there below…
From my turtle gazing on whose back I ride,
Her shimmered scales of orange shine
Neath morning's tide…

Off turtle's back I saunter a bigger fish to be,
In her seaweed peeking this little fish at me…
Reefs of colored corral sparkle 'neath the tide,
Now from our turtle gazing as hand
And hand we ride…

In silent swaying seaweed by corral all aglow,
Another fish so little lives with
Me below…

Only the dead have seen the
end of war...Plato

"Silent They The Warriors"

Fate whispers to the warrior, "You can not withstand the storm." The
warrior whispers back "I am the storm."...Jake Remington

Silent they the warriors laying sabers bare,
Fields of battle shadowed in sulphur scented air...
Notes sad of trumpets blowing as death takes them away,
Angels band together in their arms the
Warriors lay...

Mournful there Saint Michael a crown upon his head,
His hand he grips a trumpet each note another dead...
A lance upon his shoulder robed in snowy white,
Away the angels carry warriors
In the night...

A warrior silent watches thick the sulpured air,
On knees Saint Michael reaches laying sabers bare...
His face he touched with mercy in his arms he lay,
Notes sad his trumpet blowing as death
Takes him away...

Gabriel and Michael both sainted angels weep,
As notes of trumpets sounding o'er warriors as they sleep...
In fields of battle silent beneath the angels shrouds,
Sings his trumpet sadly, lost notes
Among the clouds...

Angels band together steadfast to trumpets sound,
Away they carry warriors heavenwards
They're bound...

It's so dark right now, I can't see any light around me...that's because the light is coming from you...you can't see it but everyone else can...

"Silent Trumpets Sounding"

For truly we are all angels temporarily hiding as humans…Brian Weiss

Silent trumpets sounding as heaven's angels cry,
As gathered notes of mortals fade 'neath diming sky…
Doves mourning in sweet meadows on twilight's misty eve,
Where shadowed moonlight beckons as
Heaven's angels grieve…

Silent trumpets sounding between the dark and light,
A pause of immortality known as mortals night…
As another angel newly born, winged without despair,
In Michael's hand a trumpet sounds,
Sweeping heaven's stair…

Gowned in golden satin tiny wings on shoulders bare,
Upon soft fragrant breezes flowing tresses there…
Lips blushing crimson smiling watching from afar,
Winged angels gathered singing behind
Their brightest star…

Doves mourning in sweet meadows as willows sadly weep,
Hanging heads in sorrow shy violets sadly sleep…
As gathered notes of mortals shadow heaven's star,
By Michael's side an angel,
Smiling from afar…

As another angel newly born, winged without despair,
In Michael's hand a trumpet sounds,
Sweeping heaven's stair…

Oh how beautiful am I! There is no other more beautiful than me"! Hibiscus told every flower native she met, from the does and deer, to the leaves and trees…

"Sweet Sharon Beware"

Rose of Sharon

Mother Nature tired of the vain, beautiful hibiscus and told her…"For your vanity,
your beauty will last only one day. From sun-up, you will be at your best, but
when the sun goes down, your beauty will fade as the dusk approaches"!

Sharon sweet Sharon a wreath for your head,
Fade not my beauty your blushes of red…
As late daylight ashes fragrant the air,
A flower my beauty sweet Sharon
Beware…

Cry the bells sadly dreaming of thee,
Beautiful Sharon where could you be…
Wine flavored kisses fragrant the air,
A flower your nectar sweet Sharon
Beware…

Sharon sweet Sharon in blushes once red,
Fade now your beauty no wreath for your head..
Cry the bells sadly no more with delight,
Your wine flavored kisses scent
Not the night…

As late daylight ashes fragrant the air,
Beneath your leaves dying sweet
Sharon beware…

No I would not want to live in a world without dragons, as I would not want to live in a world without magic, for that is a world without mystery…and that is a world without faith…R.A. Salvatore

"The Dragon King"

Dragons and legends…it would have been difficult for any man
not to want to fight beside a dragon…Patricia Briggs

Silver scaled with forked tail eyes a tearful green,
His woeful cries 'neath yellow'd skies in valleys never seen…
Purple winged this dragon king sad, yet eloquent,
Telling tales with fond farewells in
Days of goodness spent…

Sunsets glow while fading slow in valleys never seen,
Wings outspread he lay'd his head with eyes a tearful green…
Those days of old in stories told his fire breathing pride,
There displayed as knights were slay'd,
Searching for his bride…

With nostrils wide he held his bride ever growing still,
She breathed her last in centuries past alone on valleys hill…
Rust covered mail on dragon's tail trumpets long un-blown,
Purple'd wing this dragon king
Silent and alone…

Woeful sounds still surround in sunsets solemn trance,
Never seen these valleys green or knights with sword and lance…
Shaking hands this dragon stands his nostrils flaring wide,
I turn to leave as still he grieves…while
Searching for his bride…

Fairies ask that you breathe in and appreciate the vantage point from which you stand, then trod carefully and respectfully with each step you make across this beautiful land…Molly Friedenfeld

"The Fairies Ride"

Fairies with gossamer wings, bring forth beauty, grace and joyful things.
Fairies of the earth are caretakers of our soil, water and trees…they watch
over creatures such as bears, bunnies and bees…Molly Friedenfeld

Last night I glimpsed a fairy,
Behind an oak'n tree…
In shadows slyly watching,
A singing bumble
Bee…

Lined wings of sparkled silver,
Her dress adorned in dew…
Flashing eyes of violet,
With hair a golden
Hue…

Swaying softly to his humming,
This pretty bumble bee…
In shadows was the fairy,
Behind the oak'n
Tree…

A flickering thing in her hand,
A tiny lariat…
Around the bee a'casting,
Now caught…as in
A net…

A hustle and a bustle,
From behind that oak'n tree…
The fairy now was riding,
That pretty bumble
Bee…

The fairy poet takes a sheet of moonbeam silver white; His ink is dew from daisies sweet, his pen a point of light...Joyce Kilmer

"The Fairy Poet"

Fairies with gossamer wings, bring forth beauty, grace and joyful things...Molly Fredenfeld

In meadows greened enchanted vales,
Sleeps fairy wing'd 'neath bluing bells...
O'er silver sprinkled cockle-shells,
As fragrant breezes scent
The dales...

On shinning starlight twinkling bright,
In dewy morning's faded light...
Night-dew still where fairy lies,
In flower bed with
Sleepy eyes...

In meadows greened enchanted vales
Fairies weave their magic spells...
Painting silver cockle-shells,
The color of their bluing
Bells...

On flowers bright she rest her head,
Waking from her dewy bed...
Stories weaved in scented vales,
By sleepy fairies spinning
Tales...

All forest are one – they are all echoes
of the first forest that gave birth to
Mystery when the world began...
Charles de Lint, Spiritwalk

"The Forest Queen"

The forest was not dark, because darkness has nothing to do with the forest – the forest is made of life, of light – but the trees moved with wind and subtle creatures…Lauren Groff

In silence sleeps the forest queen,
As dark the shadows creep unseen…
Light of candle slowly wanes,
In this forest queens
Domain…

Silvered stars through canopy,
As shattered beams through oak'n tree…
Hoots an owl "forevermore"
To queen asleep on forest
Floor…

Bullish frogs expressing woe,
Reclining where the cattails grow…
Away to whisper "nevermore"
As shadows creep on
Forest floor…

Smiles moon-maiden all adore,
While tales she spins of years before…
Creatures all now gathered there,
Rabbits, wolves and grizzly
Bear…

By the sleeping forest queen,
Are angels sitting quite unseen…
Moon-maidens yarns they all adore,
As shadows creep on forest
Floor…

Midnight my friends a forest queen,
Sleeps in silence quite unseen…
Hoots an owl "forevermore"
As shadows creep on
Forest Floor…

The forest queen in shadows there,
Protects her wolves and grizzly bear…
As shattered beams through oak'n tree,
Shine silvered stars through
Canopy…

It takes courage to grow up and become who we really are…E.E. Cummings

"The Little Dragonfly"

*Deep in the sun-searched growths the dragonfly hangs like a blue
thread loosened from the sky…Dante Gabriel Rossetti*

I'm a little dragonfly,
That no one ever sees…
They always notice butterfly's,
Why not notice
Me…?

I play among the cattails,
When summer breezes blow…
Where fairies cool their tiny wings,
And fragrant violets
Grow…

I never pass a garden,
With flowers growing bright…
Upon the forest streambed,
I rest at dusk of
Night…

Unseen am I a dragonfly,
Not a humming bumble bee…
No wings of crimson beauty,
That few will ever
See…

But…God made me a dragonfly,
That few will ever see…
I may not be a butterfly,
So…a dragonfly I'll
Be…!

I have come to terms with the future;
From this day onward I will walk
easy on the earth. Plant trees. Kill no
living things. Live in harmony with all
creatures…I will restore the earth where
I am. Use no more of its resources
than I need, and listen, listen to what
it is telling me…Earth Prayers

"The Moonlight Maids"

When the animals come to us asking for our help, will we know what they are sating? When the plants speak to us in their delicate beautiful language, will we be able to hear them? When the planet herself sings to us in our dreams, will we be able to wake ourselves and act? Gary Lawless

Faded howls neath moonlit skies,
In forest deep a wolf replies…
There beyond a far-off hill,
The stalking moon pursues
Them still…

Fall of shadows dark of night,
Moon –maidens wink in morning light…
Spells they cast in timbered vales,
For howling wolves in
Distant dales…

Past mountains high and valleys low,
In summer's heat or blowing snow…
Faded howls 'neath moonlit skies,
In forest deep a wolf
Replies…

Spirits they moon-maidens keep,
In wild of night day-light weeps…
There beyond a far-off hill,
Protecting wolves and
Wildlife still…

'Neath moonlit skies howlings fade,
Cradled by the moonlight-maids…
Spells they cast in timbered vales,
For howling wolves in
Distant dales…

Poets are damned…but see with the
eyes of angels…Allen Ginsberg

"The Poet's Rhyme"

A poet's work…to name the unnamable, to point at frauds, to take sides, start
arguments, shape the world and stop it from going to sleep…Salman Rushdie

Waste not the flowers scented sweet,
Fair these petals painted red…
Blow the breezes fragrant soft,
Outside their gardens
Bed…

Waste not the notes of lyrics nigh,
Betray them not their rhyme…
Adore their music lost in air,
Together bound in
Time…

Waste not the slender junipers,
Green grows these evergreen…
Give me but their tender cones,
On mountain-tops
Unseen…

Waste not the ocean waves unfurled,
Careless they their bluing spray…
Pirates all in leagues below,
Sleep still where dolphins
Play…

Waste not the verse a poet writes,
Betray them not their time…
Give me but their tender words,
Together bound in
Rhyme…

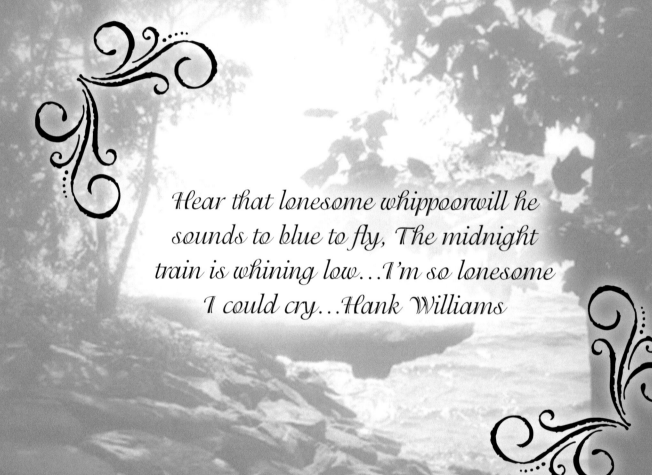

Hear that lonesome whippoorwill he
sounds to blue to fly, The midnight
train is whining low…I'm so lonesome
I could cry…Hank Williams

"The Singing Whippoorwill"

Did you ever see a robin weep when leaves begin to die? Like me, he's lost
the will to live, I'm so lonely I could cry...Hank Williams

Unto the fields, beneath the skies,
Through meadows bare and mountains high...
'Neath canopies of woodlands green,
Quiet flows the forest
Stream...

No valley, rock or yonder hill,
Hears not the singing whippoorwill...
The sea, the sea she's calling me,
In wildness there, I'd
Rather be...

Those howling winds they whisper still,
Sad faded songs of whippoorwills...
By the seas, beneath the skies,
Through meadows bare and
Mountains high...

Birds of song high in air,
O'er the fields and meadows bare...
Their symphony is calling me,
In wildness there, I'd
Rather be...

No valley, rock or yonder hill,
Hears not the singing
Whippoorwill...

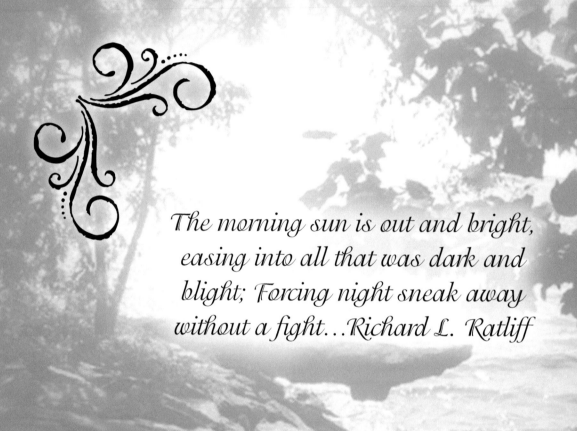

The morning sun is out and bright,
easing into all that was dark and
blight; Forcing night sneak away
without a fight...Richard L. Ratliff

"The Winking Marigold"

Open afresh your rounds of starry folds, Ye ardent Marigolds...John Keats

My friend awake with morning's rise,
As Mary winks her golden eyes...
Sing the birds in twilight's dew,
Counsels they each day
Anew...

Shadows they each murmured say,
Fading yet this dawning's day...
"Sleep ye not with morning's rise"
As Mary winks her
Golden eyes...

Pale are streams in meadows green,
Stealing night away unseen...
Triumphant sunbeams all aglow,
As flowers wake the
Shadows go...

Yellowed bright with golden eyes,
As Mary winks with morning's rise...
My friend awake this dawning day,
"Sleep ye not" the morn
Away...

Tell me the story…About how the sun loved the moon so much that she died every night…just to let him breath…Hanako Ishii

"The Wolf-Moon Beckons"

There are nights when the wolves are silent and only the moon howls…George Carlin

Cuckoo-birds and sparrows fairies silvered wing,
Heavenward while watching silent far-off things…
Trembles Mother Nature motionless and still,
Moon-maiden peeping shyly over
Yonder hill…

There beyond tomorrow yesterday denies,
Cuckoo-birds and sparrows with fairies in disguise,
Watch moon-maiden peeping o'er the yonder hill,
Heavenwards she's climbing motionless
And still…

There beyond tomorrow strikes the midnight hour,
Trembles Mother Nature at moon-maidens power…
Angry seas awaken crashing they to shore,
Bright the Wolf-moon beckons never
As before…

Cast the shadows lightly by moon-maidens sphere,
Cuckoo-birds and sparrows with fairies far and near…
Tremble in the darkness by an angry shore,
As bright the Wolf-moon beckons never
As before…

Heavenward while watching striking midnight's hour,
Mother Nature trembles at
Moon-maidens
Power…

*A friend is one of the nicest things
to have and the nicest things
to be…Winnie the Pooh*

"There Beyond"

The only way to have a friend is to be one…Ralph Waldo Emerson

There beyond a little frog alone he croaks 'neath swollen logs,
Where he thinks are other frogs here alone in swampy bogs…
Shine the stars in distant sky as wonders he "who am I",
Swim did he as tadpoles swim now alone
A saddened him…

This frog alone there beyond wants nothing than a happy home,
From forest still echoed croaks saddened still the frog alone…
As twilight yawns wakes the morn darkness leaves day is born,
Not so bad thought the frog around he looks
At other's logs…

In the pond a tadpole swims with a smile a little while,
There beyond our little frog to tadpole waves with a smile…
Croaking frogs from distant logs echo now from swampy bogs,
Alone not he, our little frog no more alone
Neath swollen logs…

With a wave a tadpole smiled to frog alone for awhile,
"Who am I" asked tiny frog, "I'm tadpoles friend!!!
With wave and smile…

There beyond a friend or foe in bog or home or all alone,
A smile and wave to friend or foe warms the heart
Warms the home…

"O Soul," I said, "Have you no tears?
Was not the body dear to you? I heard my
soul say carelessly, "The myrtle flowers
will grow more blue..." Sara Teasdale

"When Flowers Die"

God will reward you, he said. "you must be an angel since you care for flowers"…Victor Hugo

I see God in a flower,
Each sunrise and twilight's hour…
In country green or tropic glade,
Among the trees or
Quiet shade…

As scented winds in summer's sky,
Away on wings His angels fly…
Kissing earth each dawning morn,
As flowers die another's
Born…

Fade the rose with petals red,
In winters cold and snowy bed…
Away on wings His angels fly,
Yet God is there when
Flowers die…

Sunrise mourns each passing night,
While kissing earth with yellow'd light…
Away on wings His angels cry,
Yet God is there when
Twilight dies…

Each passing night His voice I hear,
Holding dear each flower near…
Away on wings His angels fly,
Yet God is there when
Flowers die…

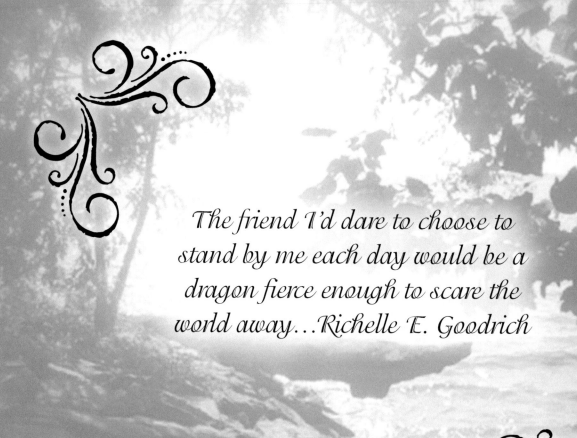

The friend I'd dare to choose to stand by me each day would be a dragon fierce enough to scare the world away…Richelle E. Goodrich

"Where Dragons Fly"

*Puff the magic dragon lived by the sea, and frolicked in the Autumn
mist in a land called Honah Lee...Peter Yarrow*

*Beware! Beware! A dragon there,
Asleep in light of day...
Close I creep where he lay,
Eyes sad that once
Were gay...*

*Awake from dreams of long ago,
O'er fields of village green...
Flare of nostrils fire red,
With his dragon
Queen...*

*Pointing he his beating heart,
Once an arrow found...
Scales of silver tarnished,
His queen no more
Around...*

*Lay there he two centuries past,
By seas 'neath starry skies...
Dreaming of his dragon queen,
Where by her grave
He lies...*

*Asleep he falls to dream at last,
By seas where dragons die...
Together now his queen and he,
In dreams where
Dragons
Fly...*

Printed in the United States
By Bookmasters